The Forward book of poetry
2005

The Forward book of poetry
2005

FORWARD
LONDON

First published in Great Britain by
Forward Ltd · 84–86 Regent Street · London W1B 5DD
in association with
Faber and Faber · 3 Queen Square · London WC1N 3AU

ISBN 0 571 22657 4 (paperback)

Reprographics by Zebra
Printed by Bath Press Ltd
Lower Bristol Road · Bath BA2 3BL · UK

A CIP catalogue reference for this book
is available at the British Library.

To Ed Victor

Preface

IMMERSING MYSELF in the large box of books and proofs that represents this year's shortlisted and highly commended poems I came to two conclusions: that I am very relieved it has fallen to Lavinia Greenlaw and her fellow judges and not myself to choose the final winners, and that the poetic voice in English has surely never been more varied.

Poets from the outer reaches of Britain, especially Scotland and Ireland, have always been strongly represented, but today's poets speak in accents from far further afield than the broad brogue heard behind Roddy Lumsden's larder door (see page 96). The seventy poems in this small selection alone draw on experiences and traditions from France and Bosnia, from India, sub-Saharan Africa and across the Atlantic. A rich heritage indeed that can encompass such different cadences and cultures.

Poetry spreads not only across cultures but down the generations. In June the list of Next Generation Poets was announced. This once-in-a-decade event promotes the most significant new voices in contemporary poetry, introducing poetry-lovers to new poets and new readers to good poetry. Our chief of judges, Lavinia Greenlaw, was one of the twenty original New Generation Poets in 1994, and I was delighted to see one of our judges, Patience Agbabi, on this prestigious new list. Several more of the Next Generation are featured in the pages that follow – indeed, Leontia Flynn and Jacob Polley are both contenders in this year's very strong shortlist for Best First Collection.

My thanks and admiration go to our perspicacious and patient judges: Lavinia Greenlaw (in the chair), Patience Agbabi, Tim Dee, Ruth Fainlight and W N Herbert. And my gratitude, as ever, to the many people who have helped bring this annual anthology into being, including Felix Dennis, Gary McKeone and his team at Arts Council England, Jules Mann and her team at The Poetry Society, our partners at Faber and Faber and the BBC, Dotti Irving, Liz Sich, Sophie Rochester, Truda Spruyt and Kate Wright-Morris at Colman Getty and, of course, everyone at Forward.

William Sieghart

Foreword

WHEN WE TALK RATHER than write about poetry, we are more likely to say what we mean. Once the page looms, we tend to lapse into terminology, a ready-made tone and a ticklish kind of semaphore. During this judging process, I have enjoyed the language used by my comrades, in particular its immediacy and physicality.

We worried about things like 'the worked-at-ness of the language' and 'the impoverishment of endings'; or that something was 'too actorish' or 'too glittery'. One poet was described as 'staggering about' and another as 'reversing out of their own poems'. Other submissions had a 'fringy feel' or were 'formally limp', and the question was asked: 'How well does it stick?' There were 'druggy poems born of staring at Raphael's blues or Giotto's ochres', 'foot-in-mouth poems' and those which were 'a distillate of poetry'. One poet's metrics were 'all shot to pieces', another's effects 'hurried, breathless and newsy'. One poet kept 'standing in the way' while another's work was 'hard to touch or be touched by'. The highest compliments were simply put: 'Dazzlingly there'.

Wallace Stevens said that we read poetry with our nerves and it is that highly attuned yet visceral condition of reception that I so enjoyed hearing described. It could be a matter of tension or oscillation, shiver or fright, the micro-effects of language or the avalanche of an idea. We weighed one poet's accomplishment against another's daring, one's sound against another's sense, but we were looking for something as coherent as it was dynamic, and the works that made it onto the shortlists met our expectations in all these things.

Yes, there were poems about the war in Iraq and the Twin Towers. There were too many occasional poems and oddly few about love. The mobility and acuity of twenty-first-century vision has galvanised the imagination and the most exciting work we read zoomed off into sur-reality while tapping a kind of ur-reality at the same time. Sometimes the poem did not survive the journey; sometimes imagery was reduced to imaging.

Reading en masse provided us with a diagnosis of our current weaknesses: irony and curiosity as an end rather than a means; the dead hand of proficiency; a soft spot for the anecdote or joke; and what one judge called 'a poverty of opening out'. We are more conventional than we care to admit and think it is enough to watch our protean and provisional selves wander through an eclectic, refractive everyday. It was a relief to find poems that said not 'Maybe' but 'Yes', or which suggested that we ought to, as they say, get over ourselves – poems that resisted human presence or engaged rigorously with the divine.

I would like to thank my fellow judges Patience Agbabi, Tim Dee, Ruth Fainlight and W N Herbert. They listened as carefully as they argued, and not only read but re-read and re-read. During our discussions, we rightly lost sight of the poet in order to concentrate on the poem, so it was intriguing to see the demographics. There are almost thirty years between the oldest and youngest on the best collection list and almost twenty between those listed for their first collections. Women dominated a remarkably strong year for first books, with voices already developed beyond conventional expectation and, crucially, beyond the expectations they might (conventionally) have for themselves.

A poem should be more than what it means and we were thrilled when we came across what Paul Muldoon has called 'an adventure in language'. A poem should also excite and delight, and we particularly enjoyed those that risked exorbitance and carried it off. As one of Mr Stevens' more delicious aphorisms has it: 'Parfait Martinique: coffee mousse, rum on top, a little cream on top of that.'

Lavinia Greenlaw
July 2004

Publisher Acknowledgements

Gillian Allnutt · LITERATURE IN CHILDHOOD · *Sojourner* · Bloodaxe Books

Peter Armstrong · THE FALL OF BYZANTIUM, STRANDED WEST OF BLAYDON ·
    The Capital of Nowhere · Picador

Jonathan Asser · 'DON'T TAKE YOUR LOVE TO TOWN' · *Outside the All Stars* ·
    Arc Publications

Ros Barber · I FILLED THE BATH WITH COTY L'AIMANT ·
    How Things Are on Thursday · Anvil Press

Chris Beckett · WHEELER-DEALER · *The Dog Who Thinks He's a Fish* ·
    Smith/Doorstop Books

Alison Brackenbury · LOOKING THROUGH · *Bricks and Ballads* · Carcanet Press

Sue Butler · THE MAMMOTH'S KNEE · *Vanishing Trick* · Smith/Doorstop Books

Anthony Caleshu · THE ART THIEF · *The Siege of the Body and a Brief Respite* · Salt

Kate Clanchy · LOVE · ONE, TWO · *Newborn* · Picador

Gillian Clarke · BREATHING · *Making the Beds for the Dead* · Carcanet Press

Mandy Coe · THE WEIGHT OF COWS · Dream Catcher Literary Arts

David Constantine · TRILOBITE IN THE WENLOCK SHALES · *Poetry London*

Jonathan Davidson · THE EARLY TRAIN · *Tabla Book of New Verse 04*

Jane Draycott · THE NIGHT TREE · *The Night Tree* · Carcanet Press
    (Oxford Poets)

Sasha Dugdale · AIRPORT · *Notebook* · Carcanet Press (Oxford Poets)

Carrie Etter · THE TRAPEZE ARTIST'S DEAR JOHN LETTER · *Metre*

Leontia Flynn · THE FURTHEST DISTANCES I'VE TRAVELLED · 26 · *These Days*
    Jonathan Cape

Cheryl Follon · BOASTS · *All Your Talk* · Bloodaxe Books

John Fuller · GHOSTS · *Ghosts* · Chatto & Windus

Kathryn Gray · THE BOOK OF NUMBERS · THE POCKET ANGLO-WELSH CANON ·
    The Never-Never · Seren

Vona Groarke · THE LOCAL ACCENT · *Metre*

Michael Hamburger · THE DOG-DAYS INTERRUPTED · *Wild and Wounded* · Anvil
    Press Poetry

Selima Hill · NIGHT-ROOM JUNE 12TH, NIGHT-ROOM JUNE 25TH · *Lou-Lou* · Bloodaxe Books

Matthew Hollis · THE STONEMAN · *Ground Water* · Bloodaxe Books

Paul Hyland · TERRORIST · *Art of the Impossible* · Bloodaxe Books

Kathleen Jamie · THE TREE HOUSE · SPEIRIN · *The Tree House* · Picador

John Kinsella · BALL LIGHTNING AS MEDIUM · *Lightning Tree* · Arc Publications

August Kleinzahler · THE STRANGE HOURS TRAVELERS KEEP · ON WAKING IN A ROOM AND NOT KNOWING WHERE ONE IS · *The Strange Hours Travelers Keep* · Faber and Faber

R F Langley · MY MOTH: MY SONG · Carcanet Press

Michael Laskey · THE PAIN ON HIS FACE · *Permission to Breathe* · Smith/Doorstop Books

Michael Longley · THE FRONT · WHITE WATER · *Snow Water* · Jonathan Cape

Roddy Lumsden · OVERHEARD IN A SCOTTISH LARDER · *Mischief Night* · Bloodaxe Books

Carola Luther · WALKING THE ANIMALS · THE POINT MARKED X · *Walking the Animals* · Carcanet Press

Kona Macphee · SHREW · *Tails* · Bloodaxe Books

Jack Mapanje · THE STENCH OF PORRIDGE · *The Last of the Sweet Bananas* · Bloodaxe Books

Medbh McGuckian · THE TENTH MUSE · *The Book of the Angel* · Gallery Books

Robert Minhinnick · THE CASTAWAY · *PN Review*

John Montague · THE DEER TRAP · *Drunken Sailor* · Gallery Books

Graham Mort · PIANOFORTE · *A Night on the Lash* · Seren

Daljit Nagra · LOOK WE HAVE COMING TO DOVER! · *Poetry Review*

Helena Nelson · SELF-PORTRAIT AS THE SONG OF SOLOMON · *Ambit*

Sharon Olds · ANIMAL DRESS · *Poetry London*

Leanne O'Sullivan · THE JOURNEY · *Waiting For My Clothes* · Bloodaxe Books

Ruth Padel · THE ALLIGATOR'S GREAT NEED AND GREAT DESIRE · *The Soho Leopard* · Chatto & Windus

Pascale Petit · CARVING THE DEAD ELM OF LE CAYLAR · *Poetry Wales*

Jacob Polley · THE KINGDOM OF SEDIMENT · THE GULLS · *The Brink* · Picador

Andrea Porter · HEIKE WITH HER DICTIONARIES · *The Shop*

Sheenagh Pugh · CHOCOLATE FROM THE FAMINE MUSEUM · Bridport Prize

Jeremy Reed · JOSEPHINE BAKER'S CHIC · *Duck and Sally on the Inside* ·
      Enitharmon Press

Maurice Riordan · STARS AND JASMINE · *Poetry London*

Eva Salzman · THE HAVING OF THE CAKE · *Double Crossing* · Bloodaxe Books

Ann Sansom · CROSSING THE NILE · *In Praise of Men and Other People* ·
      Bloodaxe Books

Catherine Smith · WHAT SHE SEES · *The Butcher's Hands* · Smith/Doorstop Books

Subhadassi · PEELED · *Peeled* · Arc Publications

Mario Susko · CONVERSATION · Dream Catcher Literary Arts

David Swann · TWO WINDS · Bedford Open Poetry Group

Matthew Sweeney · A DREAM OF HONEY · *Sanctuary* · Jonathan Cape

Michael Symmons Roberts · PELT · JAIRUS · *Corpus* · Jonathan Cape

Susan Wicks · NIGHT TOAD · *Night Toad* · Bloodaxe Books

C K Williams · OH · *The Singing* · Bloodaxe Books

Pat Winslow · OS · *Poetry News*

Contents

Highly Commended Poems 2004

17

Shortlisted Poems
The Forward Prize for Best Collection

Kate Clanchy

LOVE

I hadn't met his kind before.
His misericord face – really
like a joke on his father – blurred
as if from years of polish;
his hands like curled dry leaves;

the profligate heat he gave
out, gave out, his shallow,
careful breaths: I thought
his filaments would blow,
I thought he was an emperor,

dying on silk cushions.
I didn't know how to keep
him wrapped, I didn't know
how to give him suck, I had
no idea about him. At night

I tried to remember the feel
of his head on my neck, the skull
small as a cat's, the soft spot
hot as a smelted coin,
and the hair, the down, fine

as the innermost, vellum layer
of some rare snowcreature's
aureole of fur, if you could meet
such a beast, if you could
get so near. I started there.

One, Two

The camera has caught me
in a church doorway, stooping
to fasten what must be

my old cork-soled sandals,
their thick suede straps,
that dry, worn grip at heel

and instep. I'm smiling
downwards, pinkly
self-conscious, and above me

the arch is an extraordinary
blue. New – the whole place
was just lime-washed, azure

and sapphire rough-brushed
over moss. It stood in the moist heat
at a confluence of rivers –

I've even noted their names,
and the date, which says you, love,
are perhaps ten cells old.

In the humid space beneath
my dress, my body is bent
in the small effort of buckling,

the sag of my stomach briefly
leant on my thigh,
and, at the crux, in the press

of my nerveless places, you
are putting me on, easily,
the way a foot puts on a shoe.

Kathleen Jamie

THE TREE HOUSE

Hands on a low limb, I braced,
swung my feet loose, hoisted higher,
heard the town clock toll, a car
breenge home from a club
as I stooped inside. Here

I was unseeable. A bletted fruit
hung through tangled branches
just out of reach. Over house roofs:
sullen hills, the firth drained
down to sandbanks: the *Reckit Lady*, the *Shair as Daith*.

I lay to sleep,
beside me neither man
nor child, but a lichened branch
wound through the wooden chamber,
pulling it close; a complicity

like our own, when arm in arm
on the city street, we bemoan
our families, our difficult
chthonic anchorage
in the apple-sweetened earth,

without whom we might have lived
the long ebb of our mid-decades
alone in sheds and attic rooms,
awake in the moonlit souterrains
of our own minds; without whom

we might have lived
a hundred other lives,
like taxis strangers hail and hire,

that turn abruptly on the gleaming setts
and head for elsewhere.

Suppose just for the hell of it
we flagged one – what direction would we give?
Would we still be driven here,
our small-town Ithacas, our settlements
hitched tight beside the river

where we're best played out
in gardens of dockens
and lady's mantle, kids' bikes
stranded on the grass;
where we've knocked together

of planks and packing chests
a dwelling of sorts; a gall
we've asked the tree to carry
of its own dead, and every spring
to drape in leaf and blossom, like a pall.

SPEIRIN

Binna feart, hinny,
yin day we'll gang thegither
tae thae stourie
blaebellwids,
and loss wirsels –

see, I'd raither
whummel a single oor
intae the blae o thae wee flo'ers
than live fur a' eternity
in some cauld hivvin.

Wheest, nou, till I spier o ye
will ye haud wi me?

August Kleinzahler

THE STRANGE HOURS TRAVELERS KEEP

The markets never rest
Always they are somewhere in agitation
Pork bellies, titanium, winter wheat
Electromagnetic ether peppered with photons
Treasure spewing from Unisys A-15 J mainframes
Across the firmament
Soundlessly among the thunderheads and passenger jets
As they make their nightlong journeys
Across the oceans and steppes

Nebulae, incandescent frog spawn of information
Trembling in the claw of Scorpio
Not an instant, then shooting away
Like an enormous cloud of starlings

Garbage scows move slowly down the estuary
The lights of the airport pulse in morning darkness
Food trucks, propane, tortured hearts
The reticent epistemologist parks
Gets out, checks the curb, reparks
Thunder of jets
Peristalsis of great capitals

How pretty in her tartan scarf
Her ruminative frown
Ambiguity and Reason
Locked in a slow, ferocious tango
Of *if not, why not*

On Waking in a Room and Not Knowing Where One Is

There is a bureau and there is a wall
and no one is beside you.
Beyond the curtains only silence,
broken now and again by a car or truck.
And if you are very still
an occasional drip from the faucet.
Such are the room's acoustics
it is difficult to place exactly where from.
Also, the tick of the clock.
It is very dark.
There exist all manner of blacks,
lampblack, for instance,
much favored by the ancients,
so deep and dense
and free of any shades of gray
or brown. But this,
this dark is of another order,
compounded of innumerable shadows,
a weave of them.
One is able to make out shapes.
It is not restful, to be like this, here,
nor is it a fearful place.
In a moment or two you will know
exactly where you are,
on which side the door,
your wallet, your shoes,
and what today you'll have to do.

Cities each have a kind of light,
a color even,
or set of undertones
determined by the river or hills
as well as by the stone
of their countless buildings.
I cannot yet recall what city this is I'm in.
It must be close to dawn.

Michael Longley

THE FRONT

I dreamed I was marching up to the Front to die.
There were thousands of us who were going to die.
From the opposite direction, out of step, breathless,
The dead and wounded came, all younger than my son,
Among them my father who might have been my son.
'What is it like?' I shouted after the family face.
'It's cushy, mate! Cushy!' my father-son replied.

WHITE WATER
in memory of James Simmons

Jimmy, you isolated yourself
At the last bend before white water.
We should have been fat jolly poets
In some oriental print who float
Cups of warm saké to one another
On the river, and launch in paper boats
Their poems. We are all separated.
Your abandoned bivouac should be called
Something like the Orchid Pavilion.

Michael Symmons Roberts

PELT

I found the world's pelt
nailed to the picture-rail
of a box-room in a cheap hotel.

So that's why rivers dry to scabs,
that's why the grass weeps every dawn,
that's why the wind feels raw:

the earth's an open wound,
and here, its skin hangs
like a trophy, atrophied beyond all

taxidermy, shrunk into a hearth rug.
Who fleeced it?
No record in the guest-book.

No-one paid, just pocketed the blade
and walked, leaving the bed
untouched, TV pleasing itself.

Maybe there was no knife.
Maybe the world shrugs off a hide
each year to grow a fresh one.

That pelt was thick as reindeer,
so black it flashed with blue.
I tried it on, of course, but no.

JAIRUS

So, God takes your child by the hand
and pulls her from her deathbed.
He says: 'Feed her, she is ravenous.'

You give her fruits with thick hides
– pomegranate, cantaloupe –
food with weight, to keep her here.

You hope that if she eats enough
the light and dust and love
which weave the matrix of her body

will not fray, nor wear so thin
that morning sun breaks through her,
shadowless, complete.

Somehow this reanimation
has cut sharp the fear of death,
the shock of presence. Feed her

roast lamb, egg, unleavened bread:
forget the herbs, she has an aching
fast to break. Sit by her side,

split skins for her so she can gorge,
and notice how the dawn
draws colour to her just-kissed face.

Shortlisted Poems
The Felix Dennis Prize for Best First Collection

Leontia Flynn

THE FURTHEST DISTANCES I'VE TRAVELLED

Like many folk, when first I saddled a rucksack,
feeling its weight on my back –
the way my spine
curved under it like a meridian –

I thought: Yes. This is how
to live. On the beaten track, the sherpa pass, between
  Krakow
and Zagreb, or the Siberian white
cells of scattered airports,

it came clear as over a tannoy
that in restlessness, in anony
mity:
was some kind of destiny.

So whether it was the scare stories about Larium
– the threats of delirium
and baldness – that led me, not to a Western Union
wiring money with six words of Lithuanian,

but to this post office with a handful of bills
or a giro; and why, if I'm stuffing smalls
hastily into a holdall, I am less likely
to be catching a Greyhound from Madison to
  Milwaukee

than to be doing some overdue laundry
is really beyond me.
However,
when, during routine evictions, I discover

alien pants, cinema stubs, the throwaway
comment – on a Post-it – or a tiny stowaway
pressed flower amid bottom drawers,
I know these are my souvenirs

and, from these crushed valentines, this unravelled
sports sock, that the furthest distances I've travelled
have been those between people. And what survives
of holidaying briefly in their lives.

Last night I dreamt that I was 26,
the age my mother was when she married
and shunted from her crowded homestead in the city
into a solitary bungalow built by my father;
looking over the stubbly field she gave up
this last unholy qualm: what have I done?

My father still lived in a village in County Down
at – for him – the adolescent age of 26.
There was a long tot machine which could add up
and subtract accounts (my grandmother had married
a tradesman) at the yank of a stiff lever:
a gadget charming, he says, in its simplicity.

My parents met at a dancehall in the city.
I see her in a sleeveless dress, perhaps, sitting down
and my jug-eared and inimitable father
considering that he is no longer 26 –
he's beginning to feel the minuses of the unmarried.
He smokes the fags that later she makes him give up

and crosses the dance floor. Would my mother get up
and dance with him? Outside the city
is in darkness: industrial but unhurried.
A slight, predictable rain is falling down.
My mother, who is not yet 26,
agrees to dance one dance with my jug-eared father.

This is the turning point. This is the father
of all love stories: the moment they give up
the multiple things of life round 26.
The lights in the dancehall shift in intensity;
the mirror ball throws snowflakes in a meltdown.
26, they say, is a good age to get married

or to do something momentous like get married.
These are the past lives of my mother and father
which have come to me in fragments, handed down
like a solvable puzzle – ready to give up
some clue to the possibilities of the city
that my mother left when she was 26.

Last night I dreamt that I was 26 and married
to the city. Under a fog, the voice of my father:
What will you give up? What will be handed down?

Kathryn Gray

The last four digits of your number I can't remember:
the first might be her winning call at bingo,
some of the houses (evens on a street) I never lived in.
A pack of John Player's, then double Mahler's
whatever, the Chanel counter, acrylic sienna daubed
into an earlobe-shaped space on the canvas
or a coin produced from a sleeve, during an evening's
prestidigitation and the deck of incontinent cards
that spills and skims from the croupier's hands.
The times shuffle for each departure gate at Heathrow
or the trains on a station concourse I've memorized
in no particular order, a date for Waterloo, then the buses
tour Trafalgar Square, the total degrees to all those angles,
collapsed roughly to the Equator, tiers becoming slices
of wedding cake; the vital percent off that dress,
without which no man can buy or sell, or else a tetragram,
which brings me back more or less to what I mean,
the last four digits of your number I can't remember.

THE POCKET ANGLO-WELSH CANON

One day, you and I will walk the aisles of libraries,
with their plausible stink of the shut generations,
to pass over an entire canon that's long been thumbed
to stub and take from some or other imagined shelf
the intimate apocrypha.
                              Cloth binding
will be the opened-out in prayer, the warp of weather
down the stone and across denominations, where air
is more than lost, gone a pointillism of coal dust. I mean
the cant of the great and good who never made us famous,
and in the first language, namely *English*. And I swear
that though these words were never ours,
they will have happened like a history, share that taste
of copper on the tongue, have a certain easiness
with human heat; they'll be the pure that's cast
by men in ballots, a pickling of steel.
How the negative was to right the light from dark,
the schoolroom's slag-flood glare will wake dead arms.
This, the book we hold and in our hands.

Matthew Hollis

THE STONEMAN

A type, mind, is a little man;
a face, a beard, shoulders and arms,
look — even the shank of a body.
    A R Spalding, *The Mannerisms of Type*

I

A true navigator, he could course
the old print-works from memory –
decoding a world of picas and rubies,
of going to the case for brevier, bourgeois;
lining the back-to-front type, sort by sort,
or leading the galley for the optimum gauge;
before taking the chase to the stoneman
who'd dress it with furniture, sidesticks, quoins,
measuring the gutters and locking the forme for press.

A world of infinite detail, he learned
to tell founts by the slightest flourish:
the kern of an f, or the spur on a G –
those stubby descenders of Goudy,
those Baskerville *J*s, Fournier *z*s,
and the crazed swash of Caslon, Garamond.
He would scour the cases for dog's cocks, ampersands,
the Old Face of Blado-Poliphilus;
drumming-up scraps on the origins of *out of sorts*;
how we take *upper* and *lower* case
from the height at which the type was stored.

To handle the language like that –
to lift, assured, each letter into place,
knowing it either clean or dissed
(one or the other, no in-between);

and throwing the frocked type for the recast
when the paraffin no longer did the trick.

And yet, more than aware of composing a line
that would soon be lifted and distributed,
so that nothing he worked would survive him
only its residue: imposed, in print, out of it.

In the same way, his men are scattered now, far flung
or melted down, leaving only the legacy:
of how as a young devil some wag would send him
for skyhooks, striped ink, an italic space,
or the old long weight. And what after all
did the 0 say to the 8, but *I like your belt*.

II
'The, ah, thing, you know,
that goes with the mongoose,
no, mouse, no. Ah.'
                                    Again.
'The thing, *this* – '
(triangular shape w. hands)
'and the thing, *this* – '
(rectangular shape w. hands)
'and I want some. Okay?'

Far from okay, it's November
and you've talked this way since March —
raffling for nouns, what my compositor
would call *a pie*, all out of sorts,
your galley of the swapped-around.

THANK   :   GOD
how it makes you smile to hear yourself say
that you've fed the briefcase or the mantelpiece;
and, in its way, how eloquent that
booting your laptop 'manufactures the sky'.

But you're tongued-tied, belted,
deported from language, to where
'there are almost no zooms', or 'orange nose bags';
going to the place of 'the three easy ones',
the 'head-grind tea', or some such else;

and five miles out of surgery, your head still newly sewn –
'When will the stonecutter come to cut the stone?'

III
Let me set this line the way you want it,
and lay the letters you would choose –
no damaged characters or battered type
no sort in need of planing,
no widows & orphans but the right fount:
sheer measure, aligned, and no omissions.

All we want is to draw a little proof from the world;
from time to time, catch sight of ourselves
in the printer's mirror and say we set it right,
before moving on to the stoneman
to leave his indelible mark;

so that long after the inking
and the distributing of sorts
what is left is binding, an impression, and paper.

Carola Luther

WALKING THE ANIMALS

She lets out her animals down by the canal
when no one is looking. Opens the hinged
ribs under her coat saying *come on now
sweethearts, out you come, come out quickly!*

It's the giraffe she has trouble with, his neck
or his shin getting stuck in her throat,
but she hopes he'll unfold to a canter
and there'll be no vomiting. The parrot

and the carp, nippy little twisters, can tie
her in knots with their double-act around
the toes of the wordless rhinoceros
but she's not daft, she keeps her eyes

on his horn. How light she is, she has to hold
onto the branches when the cacophony starts.
What holds her attention is the fury of the midges
and the lonely way the buffaloes shake

the ground. As ever, the crippled dog howls
for his liver which was stolen at birth, accounting
for the wastes of his eyes. The sound never fills him
but makes a drone for the shrieking snakes

to rail against, the delusion of frog song, the cheetah's
weeping. Inevitably there are complaints
from frightened walkers, but they don't stay away.
Ignoring them, she hangs on tight to the afternoon

until she has coaxed the little grey bird from its hollow
and launched it westward over the water
to pull its reflection to the point
it ignites in the silence of the setting sun.

THE POINT MARKED X

We spent a long time searching for the point
marked X on the map before concluding
it was another country. It had rained
for days and the ink had run and our hands
were covered in the blood of giant mosquitoes.
Go north said Freeman, *beyond the highlands*

to where nothing breaks the expanse
of snow except oil and chromium diggers.
Samira snorted. *And gun towers guarding the fence,*
and rank upon rank of assassin! A taint
of despair was staining the air and I knew I'd be alone
when I woke, the wrong map and cold remains

of the fire my possessions. I did go north. Where else,
now the east and the west were chronicled
and the south reduced to bone. I felt a need in myself
for something to reach, a hill perhaps, a river.
My arms and legs were oozing mosquito
poison, I shook with rigor and blackwater fever.

It is hard to remember the reality of the Pole
when everything is white and the compass swinging
in circles, or lurching from left to right. To recall
at this time the passionless way you chose your goal
is unhelpful, to concede its randomness, death. You're alone:
your nose must be followed, a rhythm set up, a cheerful

version of your repetitive heart, your muffled feet.
Sound must be made in the powdery absence of sound,
you must converse with yourself, enthuse on the route,
pretend it's not luck that today you weren't food
for the wolves or the petrol bandits, picture mosquitoes
to remind yourself how bad it might be, conserve heat

by holding your skin away from your jacket,
not let yourself think that the corpse that you pass
might be the corpse you saw before, or that the socket
belongs to the eye of someone you know, instead
let your mind rest on a purpose for travelling alone
in endless white, and reach for a path in your head.

Jacob Polley

THE KINGDOM OF SEDIMENT

I

Rust seemed to bleed downstream
from dumped washing tubs and pram wheels,
the way sheep leaked poison
as they lay dead at the source,
the taste sharp as smashed glass
if you cupped hands and sipped.

Our stream smelled of pennies sweating in a fist
and ran out from behind houses
into farmland. There, we mud-pied cows,
safe on one side as the herd wobbled, shy
at the water's edge, engrossed
in its broken reflection.

Sometimes we found a door
in a field. We'd shunt it into the stream,
then follow with branches, poking it sideways,
hoping it wouldn't wedge between banks:
when it stuck, we'd dare each other to step on,
though I was sure it would swing open

under me, as doors did when I leant against them
listening in, and pitch me through to the kingdom
of sediment, where leeches bled your shins
and bicycle spokes and ragged tins
slit the balls of your feet to the bone.

II

To the sewage works at the edge of town
I was led and drowned
while my brother kicked pebbles at a can,

furious when his shots flew wide and swam
under the slurry, breaking out trapped gas
as they were sucked down.

I was drawn by sticklebacks, through overflow pipes,
picking up the accent of the current
as I babbled down arterial byways:
I found my new tongue
could run around anything.

As the youngest under
I ascended to the throne,
ruling suicides and sea-fishermen
who've stolen into fresh water
to escape the gaping spaces of the ocean.

Sometimes I caress familiar ankles.
I hold them as the feet paddle,
but my hands shatter when they climb back out;
I feel heat beneath the skin,
and long to break the surface.

My sceptre was cast from flakes of iron
and mercury, siphoned from a salmon's gills;
my robes are trimmed with white-water,
my crown inlaid with bubbles, caught
while they still held flawless pearls of breath.

My orb is a kingfisher's egg
that rolled into the water as it hatched.
The fledgling peers from the crack
or lifts half its shell and shows me wings,
sodden at its sides. It knows no grief.
I tell it stories about above.

THE GULLS

They're trying to shake themselves out of their sleeves
in the air above the bins,
their flight suddenly akin
to dangling on a coat hook
by the back of the coat you're still in.

Shortlisted Poems
The Forward Prize for Best Single Poem

David Constantine

TRILOBITE IN THE WENLOCK SHALES

When the kingfisher flitted
Under the hazels I entered again into boyhood
Over a hurrying water.

The church clock dropped the quarters nearby
And from a little school
Children hallooed like enchanted animals

But I was watching a water that shipped the wild apples
With all the time in the world
Patient as a fisher bird

In the hazel light to learn to be a finder
Of life, its mark, on a black stone
Opened like a butterfly, a soul that water,

Swaling and swaling, had let be seen.

Vona Groarke

THE LOCAL ACCENT

This river is pronounced by granite drag.
It is a matter of inflection, of knowing what
to emphasise, and what to let drift away,
just as a slipping aspen leaf makes barely a flicker,
one gaffe in the conversation between the current
and the flow; a stifled yawn, a darkness reimbursed.

While underneath, the thing that falls through shadow
is full of its own occasion. Weighty and dull,
it longs for water, the lacquer and slip of it,
the way it won't allow for brightness on its back,
but flips around to where its fall is a wet-wool,
sodden thing that will break at any moment, and undo.

Something is coming loose like aspen leaves, or froth.
Or maunder, letting itself down like rain into a river
immersed in getting on with what it separates:
the sulk of damp soil; the stiff articulation of the shore,
the giddy vowels sprayed over the drag and ebb
of voices leaking through the rain over the town.

Everything comes to a standstill under the bridge.
The town grips the river and all the words for elsewhere
or for being there have had their edges worn off
and their meanings powdered to a consonantal darkness
where they dissolve, like happenings, into traffic
and asphalt, or otherwise, in the river and its silt.

This river is pitched so far from the sea,
it announces itself in elision, as though everything
unsaid could still bed down in depth and unison,
underwriting words for going on and every other way
in and out of this one place. Excepting the blood-red
trickle of sky, and what it overrides, what slips beneath.

Robert Minhinnick

THE CASTAWAY

    Sleepless
I keep sleep in my pocket,
insomnia a sea-urchin language
and the nights strung together dried like chilies,
the red, the black, the ceaseless, the unbearable,
the darkness of chilie wombs rattling with stars.

But every night
a whale in the bay
spits at the moon.
Though it does not exist
how quickly I put my serenade together
for our low-tide rendezvous.

Look at me, I say to the no one there.
One day these bones will be silver in the sea-holly.
But today I darken, I darken,
my skin a caste-marked congregation in a chancel of salt.

The town astronomers
are camped upon the dune
measuring Mars as it rides over Somerset.
Maybe I should throw my spear at them
or serve rainwater in an oystershell.

Such a current.
I call it El Generalissimo –
for only the current can say
where the disappeared people have gone.

I fear lightning, jellyfish, the uncomprehending mind, call
centres, ticks, the data protection act search parties
autopsy, sandfleas, journalism, tourists, tiger sharks

whirlpools, translation, the storm ten miles offshore whose
ziggurat is built from one billion tons of rain, rain bricks,
imperial staterooms of rain with rain's imperial family
waving from their balcony overhead.

Was it for this I bartered
my breath? But at dawn a footprint,
and in twilight a crab army
circumnavigates the camp.
   Meanwhile, I'm refining
my religion.
         To hell
with the sutras of sand:
every day that gospel changes.
My latest god is the driftwood god and I am driftwood's
                        dizziest disciple.
See his altars with their pilot-lights ablaze upon the tide.

My mermaid I made of marram
the storm stole, she lifted, green
grass angel over the point,
not an outline left of her
or a trace of the garden I trod her in the chalk,
and after weeks waiting not a word to her
guardian of the one who ascended
without sin or sign, my
wife from the midden,
my wife in mid
air.

One thing I know.
The cormorant is always
black. But not blacker
than the blacknesses the ocean will become:
and even the cormorant's eye will be black that an hour ago
was the Peruvian gold of Mars as it scorched the sky.

Destiny, they say,
is all: our pre-natal
navigation. So the poet sets out
over the shelves of Spezia
and there's my mother madcap on the shore
sewing his shipwreck into a shroud.

Every day
the sea smells stronger on my skin.
   At last I am utterly clean,
anointed with crow feathers, battery
acid, the fair's cinnamon doughnuts,
sulphur in the dune-rift and fire
from the fumeroles on the seabed.
How my blood rings against salt's armour.

So,
which sea tonight?
The waif?
The wolf?
Yes.

Traeth yr Afon low tide:
   the beach a looted exchequer;
   barbarians streaming away.
   I start again.

Now the current is dark and all its candles
pinched, its voices vanished like so many
voices that failed at midnight, and the sea's library
in darkness, in its greatest darkness, every book of it
and every page fused to blackness, every word and signature
translated into the language of the dark.

Patience he played
and patience he showed.
I'll show him patience, that no one there.
Here's the wayfarer tree upon the shore –
as if my father had left his diamonds and spades
all over the beach.

      August
I'm spending under a hunter's moon.
   Tides come in like brickdust,
and all the sprockled moths mad in the wall rocket.
   Sometimes I lie on the seabed
   to look at the sun.
And sometimes I think drowning's
   a white door
   behind a white
   door where a fire
   burns on a dark
     isthmus.

     First
there is an island
      then
there is no island
      then
there is.
     Or:
a sleeper in the ocean
who rises and
       shakes himself
out of his limestone trance
      every eleven hours.

  In my own dream
    I was a glass
statue on the sand with the sea
suspicious behind the mist.

And in my glass belly
beat the last
        Adonis of the dunes,
the last thought I would ever have,
        the last creature I could dare to be.
        I stood,
a statue on a shell-dust plinth,
the invisible ocean's foam
to my femurs, and the butterfly
tormented in the glass web
        of my veins.

    They told me not to swim
at night, but the cormorant is a great cartographer
and I follow the compass in his heart.
    Yet who knows these roads like me?
I put out my hand and the darkness pulls me in
and I join the army of the invisibles
whose breath is black, whose blood is black
and whose wine is the colour of the waters under the waters.
                They are waiting for me
                in the amnesiac room:
they are waiting for me to open my black mouth
and tell them all I have learned of the collision of midnights,
of the sea's unseen catastrophes.

    My sentry
is the mullein in its greatcoat.
And strange – the sea going out and going
out and going beyond me somehow,
so in place of the garden where I floated
    – nose and ears stoppered by the waves' pollen –
lie the bureaucracies of mud
    and a conger family
        fletched like school railings.

Television people come to ask
what I eat. Only oysters
oiled with samphire, I say:
or fennel's green shuttlecocks;
maybe kedgeree of seabass seared on a basket of kale.
(More truthfully scroungings from the wheelie at the
                                        Seagull Room).
Now I'm planning my own series after the soaps.

But the current insists.
Over the shoulder of tho world it comes.
And I who was sealed
am a honeycomb.

A long way out.
                    Oh never so far.
Over my head the butterfly is moving
away from the citadel and its arcades.
    Not that way, I want to shout,
that way is twenty miles without an orchid mouth.
But there it goes, as if it knew what I do not –
    black through my squint
and trembling
    like a sunspot.

Yes, I bartered my breath
for this. Here the sea's anaerobic
clerks tend their screens, every
molecule awarded its place,
never ending their trials at the terminals.

And the sea drinks with me bringing cup after cup.
What a night we have together rolling in one another's arms.
But drowning's the second
impermissible dream. Each wave is a flume
and a fugue, high pressure August swell lifting me light
as the whipweed till each wave is a fog of dirty gold

where the swimmers are smiling with their cuttle teeth
and then each wave is a child at my ankle and then a
                              mother to my mouth.
For her salt milk will make me strong as starfish,
as dead men's ropes, and I'm a belly bursting like a hot
                              Dominican plum.
Here's the wine I wanted most and never was allowed.

Daljit Nagra

Look We Have Coming to Dover!

So various, so beautiful, so new –
    Matthew Arnold, 'Dover Beach'

Stowed in the sea to invade
the lash alfresco of a diesel-breeze
ratcheting speed into the tide with brunt
gobfuls of surf phlegmed by cushy,
come-and-go tourists prow'd on the cruisers, lording the waves.

Seagull and shoal life bletching
vexed blarnies at our camouflage past
the vast crumble of scummed cliffs.
Thunder in its bluster unbladdering yobbish
rain and wind on our escape, hutched in a Bedford van.

Seasons or years we reap
inland, unclocked by the national cyc
or a stab in the back, teemed for breathing
sweeps of grass through the whistling asthma
of parks, burdened, hushed, poling sparks across pylon and pylon.

Swarms of us, grafting
in the black within shot of the moon's spotlight,
banking on the miracle of sun to span
its rainbow, passport us to life. Only then
can it be human to bare-faced, hoick ourselves for the clear.

Imagine my love and I,
and our sundry others, blared in the cash
of our beeswax'd cars, our crash clothes,
free, as we sip from an unparasol'd table
babbling our lingoes, flecked by the chalk of Britannia.

Mario Susko

I came upon a man in black who sat on a tank,
tending his sheep that grazed impassively
around the craters and among dead bodies.

I am looking for my son, I said squinting.
The bullets in his cartridge belt slung
over his shoulder shone in the sun like teeth.

He smiled, chewing a cigarette at the other
corner of his mouth, and motioned with his hand
to the field. Plenty to choose from, he said.

The sheep were moving away
towards the shade of a big oak tree,
I strained to hear the bell I knew.

He slid down and stared at me.
Is that your stomach growling, he asked.
I am just trying to find my son, I whispered.

You want me to shoot one? He spat out the butt
and stomped it with his boot that was like my son's.
We are talking about good meat, he grinned.

The shirt looked familiar, but I couldn't tell.
My sheep started to fan out and I suddenly heard
a dog yelp. He whistled, the sound

thin and piercing, making the sheep stop.
I felt the sweat run down my buttocks and legs,
as if someone was punching holes in my ribs.

Have you seen my son, I uttered, not knowing
whether any sound left my mouth. You never had
a son, he yelled and cocked his submachine gun.

The boots were the same, and so was the shirt.
And the Mickey Mouse watch on his wrist.
Tell you what, he said and laughed. I'll be your son.

Highly Commended Poems
2004

Gillian Allnutt

LITERATURE IN CHILDHOOD

What was literature?

It was, like a dustsheet, shelter.

It was instead of a father. *Wait till your father gets home.*

Instead of a mother, washing alone.

Even instead of a grandmother.

In it there was no war we'd have to keep on trying to get over.

No corridors in literature, no nuns.

All the time, outside literature, fear was going on.

There were sandwiches, Marmite usually, Spam.

Peter Armstrong

THE FALL OF BYZANTIUM,
STRANDED WEST OF BLAYDON
(for Arriva Trains)

I summon here the guardians of decline:
the sad Comneni, the half-wit house of Angelus,
the great and hopeless Paleologi
who, fitterless, must occupy
a singing throne gone dumb
(Apostles' equals, scavenging for scraps)

as we, all sweat and outbreathed air
must wait another hour and watch
the vacant track-beds settle,
the foxgloves edge towards us,
till train, till track, till town, till age
are given to the river or the moss.

Drivers and conductors
dispute the *filioque*
– *regulator* in the Latin wanting
certain finer points of Greek –
and we pray for a man with a spanner,
approaching (please God) as we speak

from Carlisle or from Venice
and their gold-rich saving West.
But hour succumbs to hour, and soon
the sky will surely lighten
on the last day of an empire
and the cut of the sickle moon.

The bindweed and the willowherb
will have scrawled across the Land Walls
or the line been axed beneath us;

bugle, buttercup, bitter vetch
have twined around your heel
and pulled.

That the janissaries of green
might wash to the essential
this that cannot now recover
– icon, railhead, porphyry;
the gleaming arcane mechanisms
that imaged a Prime Mover –

disembark, citizens.
Descend these embankments
of cinders and bracken
to where the walls stand open
on a different country
and the skylarks rising.

Jonathan Asser

'Don't Take Your Love to Town'

Nose-ringed romancers and GBH hopefuls
are making a comeback, enjoying their Friday
and murdering country-and-western emotions
which feature: Jolene, boots, a blanket, some track
laid across Arizona, Vietnam, whitewall tyres
and various buddies who won't let you down
and some others who might. You can revel in cacti
and wind effects, bushes that tumble for miles
between towns – even though this is Camden, and Deborah's
lizard-skin blouse is unravelling on Bryan,
a boy half her age playing pool, who's got plans
for her niece pulling pints. Arrows chucked miss the double,
the board even, failing to cling to the plywood
surround and then pricking the crusty Axminster
that's crocheted with roaches, just missing a greyhound
whose nerve nonetheless is intact. The fruit machine's
flashing and no one is interested. Anyone
counting on not getting smashed in the hour
before time is in danger of missing a stab
at being present that's aimed in the general direction
of love, or, if it kicks off, hate. Bryan's shoulders
are now being massaged, he's focused on stripes
and ignoring the feeling. His stepbrother, Euan,
an upended cue to his mouth, is psyched up
for a session with ex, Isobel, on the mic
and committed to doing full justice to 'Ruby' –
especially the bit where the veteran thinks
about shooting her down, if his legs only worked.

Ros Barber

I Filled the Bath with Coty L'Aimant

I wanted to smell sweet. Arthur was calling.
Sweet, sweet William. Not mine, you know.

'Nanny Jill,' he said. 'Where are you going, Nanny Jill?'
'The Palladium,' I said. The Palladium.

What a treat. Arthur was calling, see.
I had that Friday off. My birthday.

Twenty-three. I ran the hot water
first because it ran cold so quickly.

So quickly. Little William, sweet William.
'Goodbye, Nanny Jill,' he said, and I corrected him.

'Goodnight, William,' I said. 'It's good*night*.'
My sweetheart was calling for me,

I hadn't much time, had to iron
my dress. Blue it was, with daisies

and a white collar. Blue. Skin. Like – like –
Oh my little William. But he was all

tucked up see, all tucked up, I tucked him up
and filled the bath with Coty L'Aimant.

Ran the hot water first, went to iron –
my dress – blue with daisies, blue.

Skin, like – like curd.
One second, and you're in darkness.

No going back, can't have it back.
One second that could have been different.

My life is worth nothing:
that's what they think, these folk

that drop coins into my blanket.
Buy a life.

But I had a life.
I left it behind, is all.

In that second,
the one I couldn't get back to.

Because you can't go back.
And you can't close your eyes.

There's the screaming, see.
The screaming. I knew, I knew, I knew –

too late. Just a second, William.
Just a second.

Darkness.
Blue.

Skin.
He'd had his bath. I don't know why.

I don't know why he did it.
His skin was all there.

In the bath. Not on him.
Little thing. Sloughed off

like, like curd.
That smell.

Coty L'Aimant.
The heat.

I wanted to smell sweet.
Sweet William.

It ran cold so quickly.
Arthur was calling, see.

The Palladium. Blue daisies.
'Goodbye Nanny Jill,' he had said to me.

And I corrected him.
I corrected him.

Chris Beckett

WHEELER-DEALER

What do you do? people ask me at parties
so I tell them straight I'm a wheeler-dealer,

not that I deal in wheels, but my deals
have many spokes, they take the toughest hills,

the steepest valleys in their stride,
and sometimes they turn so fast I feel blood

whistle in my veins and my nimble bottom
chafing on its poky posture-pedic saddle,

I grip two phones like handlebars and race
towards the line, a ticker-tape reception

of me madly waving my arms and shouting
like I've just invented the wheel –

and not that bumpy Fred Flintstone type of wheel,
but a sleek ferocious mesh of metal rods,

with the tiniest strip of rubber burning the asphalt,
like a plaster torn off a scratched knee,

like the word YES written in smoking sulphur
in the middle of a perfect circle,

like Leonardo's perfect man stretched
to the limits of his circle, and still turning.

Alison Brackenbury

Looking Through

I read newspapers, endlessly,
when I should be doing
so many things. The actresses are best
in the obituaries: their tiny bones,
their triple marriages. How often they end up
With a dog, upon a ranch, alone.

What does this tell me, about women,
even about dogs? Nothing.
It is the soul
Which loves to look at mountains, in clear air.

Sue Butler

THE MAMMOTH'S KNEE

I place my finger in the knee joint,
not like Thomas because I doubt
but because there is no one around.

It emerges the colour of rye bread,
fermented and sour.

The joint is worn smooth,
arthritic as the swollen hands of Titian
who smeared the paint with his palms
when he could no longer hold a brush.

I like Titian
and Raphael's beardless Joseph.

Mammoth stays silent.
I have a jar of boiled water
but he is dry. No skin. No cartilage.
His eyes were pecked out by birds
I can imagine but not name.

The void of his ear cavity is impossibly large.
Can it be he listened for pleasure?

In the basement, without fuss,
Sergei corrects his young apprentice,
teaches him how to stitch lion fur
so it holds but does not show.

Back by mammoth,
a son takes a photograph of his father.
When the film is developed
they will see my face
watching through the rib cage.

I leave when the radiator
starts to burn my back.
The lobby smells of pork fat.
It is a relief to be out in the rain.

Anthony Caleshu

THE ART THIEF

You do not start out as an art thief. You turn to art
because it is worth more than televisions and safer than banks,
with their armed guards and managers, each with a necessary key.
Art you can see, and not in any vault, but hanging like fruit
in a low tree. Art is not forbidden. No god is watching.
You don't even need to wear a mask. This is what you are told,
and what you tell yourself, in between long hard looks
and squint-eyed glances, in study at the Fine Arts Museum.

You appreciate daily to make up for lost time.
You sit in on talks to sixth graders by museum docents.
You spend long hours standing in front of paintings –
side-stepping, back stepping – until you feel their pomp snap,
like junkyard dogs, their bogus façade of posture
broken … until they trust you.
Soon you can see, by the way the ballerina cranes her leg,
she always wanted a voyeur. Soon you can tell,
by the way the flowers look heavily to the sky,
their turning to the sun is really a turning toward you.

Gillian Clarke

BREATHING

Prowl the house sniffing out gas leaks,
a cloth festering somewhere,
spilt milk, cat-piss, drains.

Such talent needs exercise.
Putting the cat out, inhale her musk
as she pours herself into the night

like your long ago mother, her fur, her Chanel Number 5,
before the whiff of a moonlighting fox,
and frost, and the coats in the hall.

Some smells are faint, the distinct breath
of tap water from each place you have lived,
the twig of witch hazel two rooms away.

Some are stolen like honey, the secretive salts
of skin, in Waterstone's, say, or the bank,
as you lean together, breathing.

Or the new-born that smell like the sea
and the darkness we came from, that gasp
of the drowned in a breaking wave.

Mandy Coe

The Weight of Cows

Cows are impossibly heavy,
they are the dark matter
that astrophysicists talk of.
All the weight of the universe
can be accounted for, if
you include cows.

It is this weight that splays
hooves, deep into the mud,
draws milk down to bursting
udders, makes cow pats slap
the earth with uncanny force.

Even milked-out
they move heavily. Arching
knuckled backs under the sting
of the auctioneer's stick, they buckle
and stagger as if their very bones
are recast from bedsteads
or rusted park railings.

To see a cow hoisted
into the air by one hind leg
is to witness
the death of a planet.

Jonathan Davidson

The Early Train

Leaving the house in half-dark, I am going
without goodbye into the colder world.

During the night, at two and three o'clock,
the four year old and the seven year old

slid into our broad bed. We all slept
in the same moonlight from the street lamp

marooned across the bay from our harbour.
And the sea of leaves tugged by a huge fetch

made the noise of a squall and filled up all
our sleeping heads. And as the night went out

scouring the temporary channels of dreams,
we would, one by one, wake up. I was first.

And before I left to cycle to the station
for the early train, I photographed the three

who remained – sodium-lit in the five-thirty light –
to remember their bodies, tumbled in bedclothes,

to remember their beings, their voices and gestures,
washed up on the further shore, to remember

what it was we became when we lived together.

Jane Draycott

THE NIGHT TREE

Secondly there are the beams or sails
sometimes called petals or branches
which on account of their reaching out
through all the timetables of dark
we are forever working to maintain
and which passing vessels have likened
to the after-death appearances of saints
or the ashes of great seafarers set up
as a beacon at the gate of a new land
where like a mermaid a ship
would be surely certain to founder.

Next there is ourselves, each man
on his watch for the deception of fog
or shudder of the tower,
each keeping awake in his turn
for the sake of the light by his reading
of Plutarch's *Parallel Lives*, our one book
relayed on the stairs between watches,
or else in the pinning of moths flattened
like leaves on the lantern whose wings
like a searchlight come sweeping our walls
finding each of us out in our beds.

But first as I say there is the sea
which is a forest, our blades
cutting through like a photograph,
a sequence of light and dark pathways,
hourglasses, rain, where time travels slowly
as if at great height or in exile and men
report voices heard crying in darkness,
though for myself I think it is only the seals
calling to each other in their language
through all the leafiness of the night.

Sasha Dugdale

AIRPORT

They were sitting in the airport when the last stragglers left.
All around it was snowing, that thick, unceasing snow
That lodges on windowsills, rising up glass walls,
Rests blankly on the curves of the planes below.

He was in the middle. To his right his wife leans against him
Her coat around her shoulders, her eyes shut. Motionless
But not asleep. Waiting and calculating in her mind
The gap between heaven and earth, the hours of stillness.

Nor is he asleep. He looks down at his shirt. Grey
With specks of packing case dust. He is unshaven and aches
With the passing night and the reflected white of the ground.
He is absorbed by the passage of the snowflakes.

The girl on the left has her head in his lap, her knees
Bent up on the metal seat. She has struggled around
Onto her back and lies there looking up at the great fan
Which, despite the cold, wheels slowly and without a sound.

She seems a mere paper thing, the shadows of the blades
Are sending dark lines across her face. He has his hand on her brow
The other hand clutching gently at his wife's far sleeve.
She rests against him, his hand cups her elbow.

They come from some place closer to the centre of the earth
And appear to be waiting for the passing of the snow
The three of them there, silent, blanched by light
And the blizzard, the rest remains in shadow.

Carrie Etter

THE TRAPEZE ARTIST'S DEAR JOHN LETTER

I recede like a vanishing point on my ribboned trapeze
and trust hamstring and calf's steady marriage
when I hang from my knees.

Physics can name the force that brings the bar back again.
I'd call it *Fortune's wheel* or Tantalus's fruit,
but then I'm the company tragedienne

as all good trapeze artists are. I no sooner arrive than leave.
I love you, I'm quitting you. I live my life between
the two meanings of cleave.

Cheryl Follon

BOASTS

Fabulla, all your talk wears me down.
In fact I feel quite stripped.
This isn't a contest of strength,
flexing your muscles or violence.
Take a lesson from the girl I love,
how my girl just *peels* my heart.

Sure, you pushed a path through the maul –
all those heavy love songs,
three dozen dancers' demands.
Sure, you came away from that fight
mopping your brow with some flirt's shirt,
while my girl just *teases* her man to the floor.

Sure, every hot-hearted available lover
wants to take you to dinner. I wonder.
And all the no-go ones as well
(that's what comes with being beautiful –
you've made that all quite clear)
while my girl *lulls* over a glass of beer.

Sure, I've heard of your legendary caresses –
heavy hands on a heavier carcass –
a fox that's slipped amongst the sheep
and wants to eat.
No, no Fabulla, look to my girl –
how she *cajoles* the shirt from off my back.

Sure, who am I to say you're telling a lie? –
all the big boasts and endless brags
concerning the hundred and one lovers
you *so* love to give us.
Fabulla, it's a pity you've got no brain,
where my girl just *coaxes* a man to learn.

John Fuller

Ghosts

1

The fire, springing to wispish life
On yesterday's raked coals, breaks out
Into its yellow authentic shapes.

The radio is building a library,
Discussing 'big-boned' minuets
Over a second breakfast tea.

Rain for the moment forbids a walk.
The hillside grasses flatten. Sheep
Graze into the frame of the window.

This, then, is the moment to
Review the images I woke with:
Human shapes with the spirit gone.

Dreams already broken when
I folded your nightdress, understanding
That cartoon symbol of the departed.

The swooping spook that certain cupboards
And staircases allow to haunt
With resentment and unfinished business.

Itself insubstantial, it
Invests sleeves with empty gestures,
Deep hems with a power to float.

But mostly troubles us with simple
Melancholy, hugging its own
Knee-hump before a fading fire

Like the girl who was a woman
Before she was old enough to look
Further than her day of pain.

2

Is it possible? Suddenly arms
And hair in the dark passageway,
A touch, and a draught of cold air?

Or the rumour of shadows against lit windows
In empty cottages on a mountain
Where night and the rain are masterful?

We can only believe in what we believe
To have been absolutely worthy
Of being somehow recoverable.

Not ourselves, certainly, existing
Nowhere but in the imagining
Of such imagining and capture.

We think of those whom we still owe
Some gesture, those we would have liked
To know, those we knew best of all.

Or is it that we have translated
Our unique consciousness into
A wish to persist and to survive?

Perhaps we are both victim and visitant,
Willing and sensuous in both roles,
Willing and fearful, like a lover?

These are chairs where the dead have suddenly
Sat bolt upright in the realisation
At once of presence and transience.

These are the shadowed ceilings where
Dreams ceased at an unfamiliar
Noise and speculation began.

These are the unoiled doors opening
On to rooms where a new consciousness
Of brief tenure sharpened the shapes

Of furniture that changed tense,
Where time that was neither night nor morning
Clung to objects that were going nowhere.

It hardly matters who felt these things,
For they are what we know we share.
The connection itself becomes the ghost.

3

And then I remembered figures falling
Willingly, escaping death
Only by freely postponing it

To take a few more breaths of their
Planet's precious gases, high-risk
Commodity eighty floors up.

And they were neither graceful nor clumsy.
They were neither living nor dead.
For this moment they lost their names.

For this moment, turning as if
Recumbent, one leg crooked as if
Finding comfort in sleeplessness,

They became simply the transient forms
Of their deliverance from being:
Handlocked divers, impossible stars.

They were arms and legs and trousers,
Already emptied, already ghosts.
They had overstayed their body's welcome.

Their city had betrayed them. Alive
Still in our sleep, they are like the damned
Spilling from an altarpiece.

Somewhere there is always ash
That has no glow or stirring in it.
Only a wind, lifting its surface.

A wind that buckets and yells across
These hills, beyond the parish, beyond
The oceans, all around the globe,

And has no notion what it can
Be chasing, or why, except that they are
Something like our vagrant thoughts,

That live in one place for a while,
And it blows them onwards and is their
Tormentor, deafening our dreams.

Michael Hamburger

THE DOG-DAYS INTERRUPTED

When in hottest July
Thunder rips the sky,
Blown grey clouds block the white,
Not quite burnt out a few red poppies loom
Among the fallen that wait
For after-life, prostrate,
Short showers too late
For all save the long-suffering to bloom,
Winds mix the season's light,
Mixed currents bring relief
To the still clinging leaf,
To fruit still filling, flower to come,
Myrtle moons budding in their darkness yet
And human sharer, grim
Before that interim.
But now the butterflies
From near-abeyance rise
Mingled, the early, late,
The commonest, the rare –
A feverish consummation
Almost too rich for buddleia-searching eyes.
This whitethroat, more inferred
Than either seen or heard,
Flits in to fit the word.
Thanks to the thunder only, winnowing,
A wane has mended, a clash has purged the air.

Selima Hill

NIGHT-ROOM, JUNE 12TH

People don't have faces anymore
and nothing here makes sense except pain
and everybody's here because they know
the only way to go is straight ahead
with nothing but a blanket
and the hush
of orifices opening and closing.

NIGHT-ROOM, JUNE 25TH

Leaving the vast and shimmering world behind me,
I find myself alone inside my hair
where, during the course of a million years or more,
tiny men with pointed hair like pins
come gliding in
in bead-encrusted ball-gowns.

Paul Hyland

TERRORIST

I know that I am beautiful
in my own beech woods,
my brush over the beechmast;
my bark out-bugles men.

Ah, to their shameful dog-packs,
the nervy beasts they ride
in their crude coats, they are kind.
I would bite the hand.

At dusk now, unearthed, soft-foot
through my own beech woods,
through grass, I thread a route;
reaching their wire, I breach it.

Here are their birds, cooped, clipped;
their nicely nurtured chicken
that one by one they cull.
They are kind to be cruel.

I'm a beast in this place
with no escape. I don't know
if it's for that, from lust,
or to teach men what is just

that I harry, hunt birds
bred in fear in this cell,
that I kill, voiding blood
and feathers and untouched dead.

My bark out-bugles men,
my brush over the beechmast;
in my own beech woods
I know that I am beautiful.

John Kinsella

Ball Lightning as Medium

You can't evoke this one in a Leyden jar
unless a car in the nightblack atmosphere
works as an electrical condenser.

That you should chance upon this phenomenon
on an outback road after a sultry day's shearing,
eyes peeled for roos so easily hypnotised

by the eyebeams of cars – taking in light
& consequently de-illumined like inverted,
candescent globes. That this phenomenon

should make itself known on a bend of road
where a mate died a couple of months back,
that out there, deep in wheat & sheep country,

where stories of fireballs crashing into sun-
dried crops & dowsing them in sparks
that start no fires are accepted as fact,

death might hover as a brilliant blue-
white ball over the road, the living passing
between worlds in an instant, leaving
an after-image burning like *déjà vu*.

R F Langley

MY MOTH: MY SONG

It goes on. Hawk moths stammer in front of
the red valerian. These words, floated
in the silence, by myself, hover close
to my thoughts. The thoughts themselves almost were
words. I think they were. I think they did. How
close is close? What colour were the moths?
There was some orange on them, and the words
were white as water. Sometimes they referred
to orange. It is difficult to say,
for instance, what it is like to hold a
field mouse in your hand. It is exactly
brown, is it? But other peoples' words come
yammering about. You have to clutch your
own, inside your hand, where something seems to
prickle like water. You make decisions.
You don't experience them. Metaphors
are only other mice. This morning there
were other butterflies. Green hairstreaks. Two
kinds of swallow-tails, flat out in hot sun.
Linnaeus bedevilled them with Homer.
A battle filled with butterflies. No red
thorax, so he said, means that these are Greeks.
Achivi. Pectore incruento.
Pat as a kiss, one settles, unnoticed,
on the rim of Nestor's chariot. It
flicks open to the page that you looked for.
Pectus maculis sanguineis. These
are Trojans who have wounded Machaon.
And Nestor tapped his horses with his whip.
Pick up our surgeon, Machaon, and drive
him to the hollow ships. Papilio
machaon. The red valerian is
a city. But it's hard to character

the whelk and drift of waves. Their eyebrows flash
metallic green. Those hairstreaks. Sometimes a
shape will follow you all day, through thickets,
disturbing the names, old indications,
the sort of education where the wit
of man is hard put to it to devise
more names. Callophrys. Beautiful eyebrows
in the bramble. Rubus. Hairstreak. Hawkmoth.
Macroglossum. Big tongues in the bedstraw.
Stellatarum. Starry, starry things. You
can be hooked all day on a dab of song.
Suddenly, in the shadow of a street
a symbol is a face held out to you,
and close enough to have immediate
significance. I will think a little
promise for you. I will wrap your cap of
ferret-skin inside your wolf pelt. I will
dump them in the tamarisk bush, till I
come back, when tonight is young, around the
corner of the not so far away, to
find, held out to me, as I expected,
waiting to be tasted, certain spoils to
make it worth my while to uncoil my tongue.

Michael Laskey

THE PAIN ON HIS FACE

Mum put her knitting down and Dad
leant forward in the big armchair
and actually cheered, the news
we were watching, in black and white:
a barrier it had taken an Englishman
to break through. And teamwork too. Brasher
set the pace for the first two laps,
Chataway replaced him and led till the bell
when Bannister went past and, somehow,
powered by the roar, accelerated,
fifty yards clear at the tape.
3 minutes 59.4 seconds.
I re-ran his day again and again:
the dispiriting rain and high winds first thing,
yet how undeterred he did his ward round
and sharpened his spikes, applied graphite
to stop the grit from the cinders sticking
and slowing him down, even so slightly;
how his legs buckled under him afterwards
as he blacked out, and they hauled him up,
hooked his arms round their necks and held him
for the camera, the pain on his face
speaking to me from by far the neatest
page in my scrapbook. Less eloquent was Dad
pinned in the doorway by Budapest,
men throwing stones at the Russian tanks,
their appeal to the west repeatedly broadcast
in broken English, till transmission stopped.
And as for our troops filing up the gang-plank
coming home from Suez – the grinning asses –
he switched them off.

Roddy Lumsden

OVERHEARD IN A SCOTTISH LARDER

Wi ma lug tae the freezin door o the larder,
I cuid hear twa voices bickerin within:
wan cries, Scotch pies, bridies an butteries.
The ither says, canon o Perthshire lamb.
The first says, truckles o hramsa an crowdie,
the ither, slabs of caboc, morven an dunlop.
Wan suggests a darn of fresh Tay-caught salmon.
The ither plumps fir a tian of sweet partan crab.

Wan screams fir black bun an petticoat tails,
the ither fir girdle scones, teabreads an bannocks.
Wan declares Drambuie cream-topped cranachan.
The ither unwraps tablet an toffee wi a coo on it.
Wan says, surely, rumbledethumps an stovies!
The ither's for bashed tatties, sybies an clapshot.
Ah'm thirsty fir Irn Bru an Red Kola, says wan.
Ah'm drier fir Deuchars an Laphroaig, goes the ither.

When wan langs fir soor plooms an Edinburgh rock,
the ither sickens fir Snowballs and Caramel Logs.
Shout aye tae inginy skirlie and mealie puddin!
Naw, taste some clootie dumplin and white puddin!
Try compote on your porridge, says the first.
Tak saut and a grummle wi yer porridge, says th'ither.
Says wan, ah'll be roastin venison the day.
Says the next, ah'm tea-smokin doos the day.

Rasps straicht fae the Carse of Gowrie, cries ane.
Rain-fed brambles fae Fife hedgerows, says the ither.
The first goes, dinnae let on what a haggis is,
the ither goes, *nivver* let on what a haggis is.
A platefu' o Scotch broth or Royal Game, mibbe?
Naw, a dish o cullen skink or cock-a-leekie!

Says wan, it'll crawl roond yer hairt lik a hairy worm.
Eat up, yer at yer blind aunties, cries the ither.

Kona Macphee

SHREW

the tapered nose, an otoscope for a wheatsheaf's ear

lips that don't meet over tiny scimitar teeth

caviar eye-dots, sunk like the knots where buttons were

four clawed feet, screwed into hooks that catch air

fur in tandem streaks of sleek and spiked cat-spit

a splut of puce intestine, looking glued on, no blood

the fine fuse of the tail, that won't be re-lit

Jack Mapanje

THE STENCH OF PORRIDGE
for Jeoff Thindwa

Why does the stench of porridge
With maggots and weevils floating,
The scorching heat trapped
Within reeking walls,
The irritation of shrilling
Cicadas and centipedes at night,
The hyenas forever *hooing*,
The scorpion's ugly sting
Splitting down the spine,
Track us wherever we hide?
Why does the daily bending
At strip searches as prison
Guards hunt the anus for
Bogus designs of our escapes,
The monthly purging with
Malaria, cholera, diarrhoea,
The poison pigeon peas,
The Sick Bay queues of skeletal
Limbs craving for vallum
To heal deadly silences –
Why does the stench of prison
Suddenly catch us like lust?
Didn't the spirit govern once for all,
The groans of prisoners dying next cell
The pangs of prisoners gone mad,
The weeping blisters on our elbows,
Knees, balls, bums, buttocks, wherever
And the blizzards blustering
The rusty tin roofs
Where helpless chickens
Drip in the storm?

For how long does this
Stench intend to trail us?
Or is it really true what they say,
'Once prisoner always prisoner' –
Why?

Medbh McGuckian

THE TENTH MUSE
We must have the arabesque of plot in order to reach the end.
  Lorca

I saw the news of his death
written in white blood
on the grass of Galicia.
It was secret, it was virtuous,
the slight lift of the rib-cage,
the air's last curves
in blood's last rooms
where he performed his dying,
the delicate bridge.

Anything but remaining quietly
in the window, wide-awake,
where daybreak does not enter
and black sounds shake
the low yellow lemons of dawn.
I used to have a sea
where the waves understood each other;
his eyes were two dancing walls
that stirred the plains

and I saw no temple in them.
Deserted blue that has no history.
This sacrament is so difficult –
now they are washing his skin
in oil of white lilies and buttermilk,
eternal skin stopping the mirror
from mirroring.
The water in which his bones
have been washed sleeps for an hour.

And now, with a brief visit
to the cathedral, they bury
his waltzing ribbons in oiled silk,
and the softest pauses
of the veins in his body
that each loved in a different way.
The coolness of reeds swaying
nowhere reaches the dark apple
of his head, his night lying face up,

no blush, ashen-maned,
camellia to be grazed on,
as if a man could outlive
or out-travel his beauty
like gardens. I know very well
that they'll give me a sleeve
or a tie with all its omens
this cavalier winter:
but I'll find him in the offertory,

unbodied arrow in a city of wells,
water-voice the equal
of the Manhattan snow,
unaware that the world is alone
in the sky's other slopes.
What a burning angel turned
to ash I seek, a double
childhood, chameleon
whose branches built a nest!

John Montague

The Deer Trap

There was a cave I visited, beside Barney Horisk's bog bank, a small wet cavern with a lattice of branches plaited over. It was near a stream, the insistent Garvaghey River, rattling over its pebbles. I would climb slowly down, and ease myself into this secret space, to sit there for hours in the semi-darkness, with shorts, and bare earth-caked feet. Crouched, legs drawn up, arms folded like fins across my narrow ribs, no sound but my own breathing; nothing to see but glints of sky through the plaited branches, and the silver scrawls of snails down the turf walls.

What was I waiting for? The surprise of a head peering in, a head wearing antlers, the crash of a companion suddenly joining me as it collapses, shuddering, to its knees? We had come on it when we were digging turf, and felt it was different, something connected with faraway times. Men had driven down from the Ministry, carrying instruments and maps, and they had declared it was a deer trap, a deer pit; perhaps from the days when the *Fianna* had hunted their quarry through the great forests?

I hear the cold metal horns, I hear the hoarse cry of the hunting pack, the halloo of men on horses. For I am the hind crouched in darkness, breath rasping, hoping they will never find me, hoping to be found. A small rain begins to trickle down my back ...

Graham Mort

Pianoforte

Big in the music business, our father
once kept thirteen pianos in the house.

People found this hard to believe, so we
pictured it for them: a house never short
of ivory or ebony, our fingers waltzing over
slave-trade arpeggios; a house where we
dined from the lid of a baby Broadwood,
skated to school on the Steinway's
borrowed castors, stood pianos on pianos –
the mini-piano inside the concert grand –
and at night whispered the scary German
consonants which captured sleep.

On winter evenings we lit candles in ornate
brass brackets, softening the rooms with
Edwardian light, with homesick songs of
patriotic loss, even employed a blind piano
tuner who only worked at night, each dawn
stepping over traps of snapped strings where
he'd tempered scales to pour cornflakes
or grill toast, the daylight he couldn't see
twisting down figured walnut legs.

My parents slept or argued or made love
on a Bechstein's broken sound-board, behind
a bedroom door of lacquered panels inlaid
with *fleur de lis*; how much of our childhood
was pianissimo, the timbre of felted hammers
falling, how much spent listening then, we never
say, hearkening for wrong chords to brood,
gather, darken the piano's terrible voice.

Helena Nelson

SELF PORTRAIT AS THE SONG OF SOLOMON

I am freckled, but comely,
    O ye daughters of Caledonia,
        as the smooth side of a fresh trout
    as the stippled flesh of a barbecued salmon.
Look not upon me, because I am freckly,
    because my genes are celtic genes.
    My mother's family were angry with me;
    because I went away to Scotland;
        but mine own country have I not kept.
A motor mechanic is my well-beloved unto me;
    he shall lie all night in our double bedroom.
My beloved is unto me as a fragrance of diesel
    in the fuel tank of an Audi.
Behold, thou art fair, my love;
    behold, thou art fair in thy red boiler suit.
Behold, thou art fair, my beloved,
    yea, my treasure:
        also our bed is king-sized.
The roof of our conservatory is glass
    and our garage non-existent.

Sharon Olds

ANIMAL DRESS

The night before she goes back to college
she goes through my sweater drawer, to see
what she likes, so when she leaves she is wearing
black wool with fuchsia creatures
knitted in, elk branched across her
chest, lamb on her stomach, cat,
ostrich. Eighteen, she's gleaming with a dry
gleam, shadow of the glisten of her birth
when she took off my body, thick coat
for the long journey. In the window of the elevator
door, I can see her amber half-profile, the
strong curves of her face, like the harvest
moon. She sets. Hum and creak of her
descent, the backstage cranking of the solar system,
the light of the car goes down like a small
calm world. Eighteen years
I have been a mother! I love being past it –
resting, watching our girl bloom.
She is probably on the train now, in her dress
like a zodiac, her body covered with the
animals that carried us in their
bodies for a thousand centuries
of sex and death, until flesh knew itself, and spoke.

Leanne O'Sullivan

THE JOURNEY

We were on a train to Cork. She was seven.
It was cold and late. We had been on the train
for three hours. She was leafing through

my biology textbook as if all those inner regions
were works of fiction. She learned how to say
epiglottis and duodenum. Then she kneeled

on the seat to stare at her body in the black window,
her fingers tracing her frame, inhaling
so deeply to push that dome up and out,

and then pulling it in until she could grasp
the curved gate of her rib cage, as if she wanted
to open up her whole breast like a trapdoor to see

the base of her life. Then she looked at my face
so severely, *Where does the baby go?* she asked
I said it grows behind your tummy, in your womb.

She took it in as if something had been thrust to her.
I could sense it slowly entering her,
and for a moment I saw it all, the promise of her,

the light fibres being spun behind her tummy,
her hips as small as two fists pressed together,
reaching back into that unripe nest,

dripping like a torch in the rain.
When she was satisfied, she curled up
on the seat the way she does when tired,

her arms like a blanket, protecting
what she did not know, the train
trembling on the outskirts of some city.

Ruth Padel

THE ALLIGATOR'S GREAT NEED AND GREAT DESIRE

To be thermally, forever, stable. (That surprised you.) Harder
                        than it seems,
  But thermo-regulation is their thing. When the air
    Is colder than the water, October to late March,
      They keep to dens below the water table.
    Away from them, caught by a cold snap, they become
Completely numb, incapable of moving. All they do is breathe
  Surface-oxygen through air-holes. Temperature is their goal,
Their god and good. During winter, they take no food.

They pick an under-hang of lake or stream which will
  Stay filled with water when the spring freshet recedes.
    Listen to Mr Ned. 'See him,' he says, 'back out of that hole
      He's making burdened with dollops of soft mud
      In his mouth and on his tail, pushing a mass of mud
With webbed hind feet. He's one busy alligator, sweeping his tail
  From side to side. And trees round gator holes grow
Darker green, their roots enriched by droppings.'

For water's everything. The darkest alligators come, thought Ned,
  From Tupelo Gum Swamp where the flow is black,
    Dyed by its maker's hand – the bark, roots, fallen leaves
      Of Tupelo Gum. Gator holes, especially of older beasts
      Who, weary, cannot want to move,
Run a long way underground. That's how they manage. They survive,
  When they can't bear what's outside. They know, whatever knowing is
For them, they'll have to face the winter. So, they dig.

Pascale Petit

CARVING THE DEAD ELM OF LE CAYLAR
The Larzac, a country of 'story solitude'.
   Paul Marres

I like to start before dawn, when the bark is still coursing with
                                        star-sap,
when I can see filaments of oxygen pour through glass leaves of
                                        the ghost-canopy,
   before the sun evaporates them.

My carved creatures talk with root tongues.
They tell me their story solitudes,
and I try to be true to them, I who have not spent my life at the
                              heart of this huge plateau,

but who can draw from the well of my soul, as from tree rings,
                              the concentric solitudes.
I release them with my mallet, in the fading moon's balm.

I draw up the toad, the cops owl, the ram, the giant Carline
                                        thistle
   opening at first light like a supernova.

I summon the bison beetle, the wild boar, the royal eagle.
They pass through the conduits of my arms and out through my
                                        fingers.

The chisel's nose smells their fears as it strokes their skins.

I work fast, before noise taints the day, attending to the silences
streaming in from the Grand Larzac Causse,
                    that gather around this elm like an axis.

My armoire, ormeau mort, engraved with an acorn from the pubescent
white oak,
a hornet's nest, a horn of plenty, an ear of wheat – all wood-quiet.
These are the forms I can name. Others my chisel shapes when I'm tired.
Then
it's as if the Larzac is working through me,
carving the mistral's masks, the night's pageant.

And the shepherd who has seen these things.
As the sun rises, the lamb he is carrying across his shoulders, grows heavy
as a dead tree.

He whispers this to me, from his place in the lower trunk, when I am
too exhausted to go on.
My body lightens then. I climb to the top of the main branch

and carve a pilot hanging naked, his feet caught by snakes, his arms
raised
as if trailing an invisible parachute,
its silks tangled in boughs of the Milky Way.

Andrea Porter

HEIKE WITH HER DICTIONARIES

Zero ego. Processor of language. Thought to word.
Word to word. Word to thought.
Trawl for inflection infecting meaning,
seeming minor, but the finer points transpose to major
in the music of translation, when you're looking for the key.

Numbering evidence from Bosnia.
Sixteen days of written statements
made to a commission in The Hague.
Four days of photographs. Forensic. Focused. No faces.
A metre stick laid beside a grave gave a sense of scale.

Tissue samples. Skulls. Bones. Buff cardboard tags on body parts.
Catalogued. Identity unknown. Shown neat rowed to the lens.
Alone in a small commercial hotel you summon other thoughts,
tell yourself the shower curtain is the colour of a silk scarf
you bought in Dublin last November, drank lukewarm herbal tea
from a mug you have carried with you since Kiev,
remember rice on a patterned plate in Cambridge,
how the weight of technical dictionaries strained
your back on the train home from Frankfurt airport.
The tiny buff tag on the tea bag caught you out.

Rewind.

J five stroke seven four nine. M eight oblique three two one.
Translate the numbers. Never stumble over one.
Pour from one jug of language to another.
Never lose a single drop of blood.
Never stop to open flood gates to unprofessional emotion.
Justice requires precision. Life is in the detail. Death is in the detail.
Fast forward. Fast fast forward.

Summered forest floor green flushed with nettles.
Ecolalia of meaning in your head, different taste in your mouth.

They brought six soldiers here. They dragged six boys here.
They executed them here. They shot them here.
Gesture left to speak.
They buried them here. They hid them here.
Gesture left to speak.
Pause. Rewind. Play Kosovo.

Sheenagh Pugh

CHOCOLATE FROM THE FAMINE MUSEUM
Strokestown, Co. Roscommon

Reading numbers on a wall,
so many thousand evicted,
exiled, starved,

soon palls. The boys are looking
for buttons to press,
and Sir's at a loss

how to bring it alive. He tries
to give them the reek
of peat smoke and lamp oil

in a cramped turf cabin,
wishing there was a replica
they could crowd into.

At every turn, language
fails him. *Starving*
means wanting dinner,

not boiling boot-leather
till you can chew it,
hoping it stays down.

They sailed to America,
he laments, to lads
who've flown there

on holiday, who make nothing
of oceans. They fidget
through the video,

dying for their reward:
the gift shop.
Their faces light up,

for the first time, at sheep
in green hats, penny whistles,
toy blackthorn sticks,

and the chocolate. Praline,
ganache, mint, mocha, truffle.
They're spoiled for choice,

their day flavoured
for ever with the velvet
dark in their mouths.

Jeremy Reed

Josephine Baker's Chic

Androgynous ZIPcode,
her mulberry lip smear
is shaped like a Parisian bridge

slung over oilily loitered water.
Her burn-a-hole through paper stare
is pantherishly feral.

She's a one-off, a cracked the mould
gold-dusted chanteuse,
her pigment-lightened powdered skin

an ethnic change over.
Hair coiffed like caviar,
her powder puff's a backstage instructor

obsessively moon-dusting hits
of chalky sparkle.
She stands men up, but falls downstairs

to meet a woman in a man's striped suit
and splashy gangster tie.
Her wardrobe's computed like Wall Street shares,

assorted furs, 2,000 stage costumes,
200 pairs of shoes, in character
64 kilos of powder.

Her sensuality's like dark chocolate:
both hands a jeweller's tray.
Framed outside the Gare du Nord
tented in a mink, that's her
in 1926, clouds parking up
in blue spaces before blowing over.

Maurice Riordan

STARS AND JASMINE

Each of them has been a god many times:
cat, hedgehog and – our summer interloper – the tortoise.
A perfect triangle, they can neither marry
nor eat one another.
And tonight they are gods
who have made us laugh
under the jasmine under the stars.

Already, the hedgehog has stolen the cat's supper
and, nonplussed, she has walked beside him
rushing headlong into the bushes.
Wisely now, she keeps an eye on him
and on the tortoise,
noisily criss-crossing the gravel.

For the cat, jasmine is white but the stars have colours.
For the hedgehog, there are no stars
only a sky of jasmine
against which he sniffs something dark,
outlined like a bird of prey.

Wisely, the tortoise ignores both jasmine and stars.
It is enough, she says, to carry the sky on your back,
a sky that is solid, mathematical, and delicately coloured,
on which someone too
has painted our neighbours' address.
Come September, we will post her through the letterbox.

Eva Salzman

The Having of the Cake

Women in their 30s aren't meant to mourn for dogs or cats.
Scorned for their deflection of ancestral destiny
and less than free, they stand there while old friends reduce them
                                                    to old bats
far in advance of any such disturbed reality.

He burdens her with images of someone gross and elderly
stuffed into short, tight skirts, accentuating all the fat,
with images of missing woman's destiny – he burdened me,
his feet up on a desk, and made his cruelty resemble tact.

The girls with babies clutch them close, and blessedly.
The boys arrange their separate lives, convenient flats
both north and south (an urban nest, a nest in the country)
and wait for 45, and newer girls with wombs entirely intact.

Please don't assume in reading this you know the facts:
that of a woman scorned, or some such tritely mournful history.
Can I explain and still refrain from tiresome, polemical tract,
myself who looks beyond that man, or before this man unhappily?

I can't stand to love a loss of self, nor stand not loving best,
                                                    devotedly,
him, with the sort of passion reason can't refract;
or him, with the sort of reason lack of passion throws at me
so bitterly, like corpses strewn across the forward path.

For the final dressing up, before I take my perfect leave,
I try on all the gloves and dresses, all the habits, all the hats
with a female's love of covering possibilities.
And I would try a thousand lives and loves as well, just like that.

Did I say female? Female to despair of all you lack?
To want forgiveness for living so imperfectly?
Did I say female, to want the knick as well as knack
of being female and astray, yet always welcomed back?

Ann Sansom

CROSSING THE NILE

A hundred times or more I've crossed just here –
these iron struts that cut the iron Humber
into silver bits, this chunk of train
chunk chunk on slats to lead us in
to long flatlands of always mist and promised rain.

You've been a few years dead, big cousin,
and I haven't missed you much, but here
I always have you in the window seat –
And that, our kid, it's called the River Nile.
I'd thought it might be sea but I was young

and you were streets ahead. Profoundly deaf
and slow at school, you turned out wise and rich,
surprising everybody with a film star wife, a Greek,
who took your every word for gospel
on the strength of your blank face. It seems

you had a way with words, a way of making magic
out of fitments, long settees and space
when crowded three-piece suites were commonplace.
I'm always pleased to hear your thickened voice,
instructive, kind and half believing in the strange.

Catherine Smith

She's sent outside while they unpack. *Go and see.*
First she sees the lizard, its back patterned like carpet,
belly pulsing faster than her breath. She sees it shoot
into a crack, swallowed by dark. Next she sees plums,

blue as day-old bruises, accepting her thumbprint,
their orange flesh slashed open by a heel. Face down
and silent in the scorched grass she watches bees
bristling the lavender to a frenzy. Dry, sullen heat

prickles at her neck and knees; she tracks a beetle
on the path, listens to the splashes and echoes
from a neighbour's pool. She sees her father's face
at a window, the sharp planes of cheek and bone

white from his indoor life. She sees him vanish.
She runs into the sudden cool of dry flagstones
and sees a puddle of clothes by a bed, pale limbs
knotted hard and hot, sudden lights behind her eyes.

Subhadassi

PEELED

an time when a said a could take all me clothes off
cos I felt so open even though it were october
an you lot took piss for a decade –
that night when a put too many mushrooms in pan
second a heard me dad reversin out o drive
an you lot came out o woodwork

an wi loads o sugar'n'milk'n'nescaf
wi downed it in a oner an got right outa there,
away from semis; through intake an golcar flats
over scar lane an onto edge
where weavers cottages windows were searin red
an a took a piss in british legion car park
an knew it were comin on cos pissin
were like growin a stalk o wheat

an across valley slawit were meltin
into marsden an pike were screechin
wi laughter an lal were goin bendy
an scad were lost as per usual an wilf cun't talk
as per usual an all shamanic gridsndots like in cave paintins
nmiros neverythinbloodyelse it seems just now
were soarin through us fields o vision

an we stopped at old sandstone steps by canal
to weigh stone that were left
an stone thatd been worn bi millions o millworkers feet
leavin a curve o empty space an wi concluded
thi were exactly equal down to a milligram

an it came on really strong as we fumbled
down t appleyards – we were talkin g force six –
an the wer police sirens hung in trees

an when we got there us lager guzzled itself in corner
so we sat on bench except scad who sat on is arse
starin down canal an saying *but where are we really*

an even though us pupils still teemed us faces
you cruelly took piss an all innocence left yer
when a said a could take all me clothes off.

Its outlived us crimped hair us docks us schoolin;
us smiths albums us girlfriends us drug habits –
in most cases us friendships.

Well, I meant it.

David Swann

Two Winds

The summer after Chernobyl, I was taking
it slow up a ladder in Sweden,
painting a family's high-gabled house.

It was easy work, save for the vertigo,
and I hit it off with the eldest son
who entertained me during rain-breaks

by calling my homeland shit. 'It's where
this rotten weather comes from!' 'Look', I said,
'you can hardly blame Britain for the wind!'

He knew better, took me to a lake – crystal-clear,
dead. Stirred its acid with a stick, looking
from his mosquito mask into my English face.

'And now there is another wind', he said.
'Now we have two winds to think about'.
Maybe I was spooked, maybe it was the height ...

... but soon after I cracked a rare old pane
with my blow-torch and was paid off.
I recall cleaning brushes one final time,

noticing little blisters on my arms. It was days
since our lakeside walk and the bites were raw
but when I asked the blackberry pickers

for advice, they only shrugged. These were new flies,
they said, flies they didn't know – and looked hard
into the rain, into the crackling brambles.

Matthew Sweeney

A DREAM OF HONEY

I dreamed that bees were extinct,
had been for decades, and honey
was a fabled memory, except for jars
hoarded by ancient, wealthy gourmets.
Honey was still on the shelves, of course –
that's what they'd named the sweet concoction
chemists had arrived at, and it sold well,
not just to those who knew no better,
and the day was coming fast when no one
alive would be able to taste the difference.

Then one Friday morning in Riga
a peasant woman arrived by horse and cart
at the old Zeppelin Hangars market
and set up her stall with jars of honey
flavoured by the various flowers. Around her
sellers of the new honey gawped, then sniffed
as she screwed the lids off, then glared
as her jars were snapped up in minutes,
and she climbed on her cart again
and let the horse take her away.

In the dream, e-mails sped everywhere
about this resurrection of honey,
and supermarket-suppliers scoured Latvia,
knocking on every door, sending helicopters
low over houses, looking for beehives,
but after a month they gave it up,
and the woman never appeared again
though rumours of her honey-selling
came over the border from Russia
and continued beyond the dream.

Susan Wicks

NIGHT TOAD

You can hardly see him –
his outline, his cold skin
almost a dead leaf,
blotched brown, dull green,
khaki. He sits so quietly
pumping his quick breath
just at the edge of water
between ruts in the path.

And suddenly he is the centre
of a cone of light
falling from the night sky –
ruts running with liquid fire,
cobwebs imprinted on black,
each grass-blade clear
and separate – until the hiss
of human life removes itself,
the air no longer creaks,
the shaking stops
and he can crawl back
to where he came from.

But what *was* this,
if it was not death?

C K Williams

Oh

Oh my, Harold Brodkey, of all people, after all this time
appearing to me,
so long after his death, so even longer since our friendship, our
last friendship,
the third or fourth, the one anyway when the ties between us
definitively frayed,
(Oh, Harold's a handful, another of his ex-friends sympathized,
to my relief);

Harold Brodkey, at a Christmas Eve dinner, of all times and
places,
because of my nephew's broken nose, of all reasons, which he
suffered in an assault,
the bone shattered, reassembled, but healing a bit out of plumb,
and when I saw him something Harold wrote came to mind,
about Marlon Brando,

how until Brando's nose was broken he'd been pretty, but after
he was beautiful,
and that's the case here, a sensitive boy now a complicatedly
handsome young man
with a sinewy edge he hadn't had, which I surely remark because
of Harold,
and if I spoke to the dead, which I don't, or not often, I might
thank him:

It's pleasant to think of you, Harold, of our good letters and
talks;
I'm sorry we didn't make it up that last time, I wanted to but I
was worn out
by your snits and rages, your mania to be unlike and greater than
anyone else,

your preemptive attacks for inadequate acknowledgment of your
genius …

But no, leave it alone, Harold's gone, truly gone, and isn't it
unforgivable, vile,
to stop loving someone, or to stop being loved; we don't mean to
lose friends,
but someone drifts off, and we let them, or they renounce us, or
we them, or we're hurt,
like flowers, for god's sake, when really we're prideful brutes, as
blunt as icebergs.

Until something like this, some Harold Brodkey wandering into
your mind,
as exasperating as ever, and, oh my, as brilliant, as charming,
unwound from his web
to confront you with how ridden you are with unthought regret,
how diminished,
how well you know you'll clunk on to the next rationalization,
the next loss, the next lie.

Pat Winslow

OS

You wake up one morning to find that someone's run a highlighter pen up the centre of your road. In the old days it was all biro marks and bits of dust, Ambre Solaire thumbprints that were hard to get rid of. The waves have gone dog-eared. Time to move on, you say. But you can't. There's the kids and school. In any case, two black chevrons block your way. They've been there since '52 when the man came to measure the hill. It's steep, he told you. Very steep. His Ford Popular broke down on a contour line. You had to tow him down. He comes back sometimes. Fond memories, he says. His is a precarious existence. He lives on a fold eleven miles away. Every now and then he falls off, loses all his friends. It takes days to find them. He hasn't seen his wife for seven years. She's on the other side, he says bitterly. One day all of this will be sea, the climatologists claim. You'll build a boat and go from white to blue and darker blue again. You'll find a grid line and follow it. 58 sounds good. 58 09. Turn south at 51. Just keep going.